... Let The Children Come

Fifty-two Object Lessons For Children In Worship

Robert B. Lantz

CSS Publishing Company, Inc., Lima, Ohio

Copyright © 1997 by
CSS Publishing Company, Inc.
Lima, Ohio

Scripture quotations are from the *Holy Bible, New International Version.* Copyright © 1973, 1978, 1984 International Bible Society. Used by permission of Zondervan Bible Publishers. All rights reserved.

Library of Congress Cataloging-in-Publication Data

Lantz, Rober B., 1929-
    —Let the children come : fifty-two object lessons for children in worship / Robert B. Lantz.
        p.   cm.
    Includes index.
        ISBN 0-7880-1059-X (pbk.)
    1. Children's sermons. 2.Object-teaching.   I. Title.
BV4315.L274   1997
252'.53—dc21   96-52554
                                                                                    CIP

This book is available in the following formats, listed by ISBN:
    0-7880-1059-X Book
    0-7880-1101-4 Mac
    0-7880-1102-2 IBM 3 1/2
    0-7880-1103-0 Sermon Prep

PRINTED IN U.S.A.

Dedication

All of these messages for children have been used in a ministry with children in worship throughout the United States, Great Britain, and New Zealand.

They are biblically based, practical, and *adaptable*. After long urging to put them into print, I have done so, with the hope that they may be used effectively with children to make the message of faith a living reality for them.

They are dedicated to all the children I have enjoyed serving over the years.

Robert B. Lantz

Table Of Contents

Some Helpful Suggestions For The Use Of These Object Lessons With Children

1. I recommend that these messages be used by the clergy when possible. I believe that spending time with the young ones helps bridge the gap that is often created by pulpit, gown, and church architecture.

2. Be natural. Allow the children to see you as a person. Encourage them to be close to you.

3. Sit on a level with the children. Don't be physically above them or intellectually "talk down" to them.

4. Don't be flustered by the natural responses to questions. Use them to make the children feel a part of the process, and good-naturedly accept interruptions within the limit of reasonable control with grace and good humor.

5. Don't be embarrassed by responses. Turn them into humor where possible, even if it is at your own expense. (The adults present will be particularly pleased with this!)

6. The objects should always be simple and inexpensive; they may even be handmade. The user should make substitutions depending on the availability of objects. (Most if not all objects may be obtained at a Bible bookstore, a Catholic bookstore, a notions store, or through a church supply catalogue.) It is important that you always have enough so that every child receives one. The retention of the message is greatly enhanced by the possession of the object.

7. Discourage grabbing by assuring that each child will get an object. Use this time to teach sharing and manners.

8. When possible avoid multicolors or various shapes to eliminate choice-making or disappointments.

9. Don't drag out the lesson. Let it be succinct, to the point, and not "preachy."

10. If you do not feel comfortable with a children's time, try it anyway. You'll grow to like it.

11. Read about storytelling and try to put the ideas in this book into your own words so that you feel comfortable with them.

12. Enjoy the children ... "of such is the Kingdom of God!"

1

New Year

Ecclesiastes 3:1-8: There is a time for everything.
Hosea 10:12: Time to seek the Lord.
2 Corinthians 6:2: Now is the acceptable time.

Object: Calendars

Good morning, boys and girls. I have a very special (watch or clock) with me today. *(Show them.)* Can you tell me what you think is special about this clock? *(Responses — a special gift, belonged to grandfather, bought in foreign country, and so forth.)* No, the thing that is special about this clock is that it tells me the proper time only twice a day! You see, it doesn't run! Well, you say, what good is a clock that doesn't work? *(Make sure you actually have one that doesn't run.)*

You see, this is my own special clock that I use when I want time to stand still. Suppose I want my birthday to last a long time or I'm late filing my tax return, or I'm enjoying a vacation, or any pleasant experience that I don't want to end.

Well, then, I just get out my trusty old clock and the hands never move. I can set them whenever I want them and time will stand still. Isn't that great? Wouldn't you like a clock or watch like that? You'd never be late for school, you'd never get up late, you'd always be on time for dinner or your chores, wouldn't you? *(Response — By this time someone will object that you can't stop time.)*

I've been very disappointed because I found that out, too! You can stop the hands of the clock but you cannot stop time. It doesn't stand still. It goes on in regular daily, weekly, monthly, yearly cycles, and none of us can stop it, even if we'd like to.

That makes me realize that time is a very precious gift that God has given to us. There is a wise word in the Bible that tells us that

9

there is a time appointed for all things, especially a time to respond to God.

As we come into a new year that God has given us, let's receive it as a gift from him and use it for our own improvement and to his glory.

Let me put the new year into your hands. *(Give calendars.)*

(Prayer for the beginning of a new year that we cannot stop or hold back but rather use to glorify God.)

2

Our Days Are In His Hands

Proverbs 3:2: Length of days and years in life.
Isaiah 61:2: Favorable year of the Lord.
Galatians 4:10: Observe days and months, and seasons of years.

Object: Yearly calendar cards

Happy New Year! That's an appropriate greeting for this time of year, isn't it, boys and girls? We all want to look forward with anticipation of happiness for ourselves and for others as well.

Why do we have a New Year's Day holiday? *(Responses may vary greatly. Aim for the idea of marking new beginnings, at least in our time accounting system.)*

We mark the passage of time by the sun and the rotation of the earth around the sun, don't we? It takes just over 364 days for the earth to complete one revolution around the center of our solar system. And we mark these annual events with a number to denote the passage of time. Who can tell me what the number of the New Year is? *(Response.)* And soon we will mark the start of a new century, won't we? Who can tell me when that will be? *(Response.)* Of course, the correct answer is 2001.

I suppose that it is good for us to have a time when we can look back at a year that has just passed and forward to a new year's beginning, so that we can see where we are in our personal lives as well as world history.

Many people take this time of year to do some very special reflecting and make some plans for the new year. Do you know what we call the plans or promises that we make at the start of the year? *(Response — Resolutions.)*

New Year's resolutions may be a good way to remind us of things we want to change in the days ahead, but it is not just at one time of year that God wants us to look at our lives and make changes.

11

He expects the process of growth and change to take place continually as we become the new people that He wants us to be as the people of his kingdom.

Here is a brand new year that I am putting into your hand. May it be happy in the Lord. *(Pass out the yearly calendars.)*

(Prayer for the opening of a new year of promise.)

3
The New Life

2 Corinthians 5:17: When someone becomes a Christian, he becomes a brand new person.

Object: Peanuts in the shell

Good morning, boys and girls. I'm going to show you something that no human being has ever seen before! Can you believe that? I have something in my hand that no one in this place has ever laid eyes on, and yet it is a very simple thing.

Any guesses this morning? *(Responses will be wild, maybe funny. Go on with it as long as you feel comfortable. Respond positively to reasonable suggestions.)*

Well, if you're ready, here it is! *(Produce a nice plump peanut. Surprise and maybe a little disappointment will be registered.)* Oh, you thought I really had something great to show you, didn't you? Well, I told you the truth; for inside this shell are peanuts that have grown there without anyone ever seeing them. Now when I crack the shell, we are going to see what no one has ever seen before — these particular peanuts. Look! *(Crack and open shell.)* Aren't they nice looking? Ummm! Good, too!

You know, the Bible talks about people becoming brand new on the inside when they become Christians. In a way that's sort of like seeing something new. God makes people new inside and they begin to show this newness in the way they live on the outside.

We can't break people open to see what they look like inside to see if they have God in their hearts, but we can often see it on the outside by the way they love other people.

Maybe we all need to be a little nuts! Brand new on the inside. *(Prayer for God to continue to make us new persons inside.)*

(Give each child a peanut in the shell. Encourage them to share the story with their friends or parents.)

4

Jonah's Disobedience And Restoration

Jonah 1:17: The Lord appointed a great fish to swallow Jonah.

Object: Whale stickers, stamps, toys, or balloons with Jonah story on them (If you live in an area where whale watching is possible, you might hold up an advertising brochure at the start.)

Good morning, boys and girls. How many of you have ever seen a whale? Either you've gone on a whale watch, or been to an aquarium like Sea World, or you have seen them on television. Anybody? *(Hands.)* Yes, I think most of us have seen whales and know that they are among the largest mammals on the earth. They live in the deep seas and oceans of the world, and although they used to be hunted for the oil that could be made from their fat, they are now protected by most nations.

There is a whale of a story in the Bible. Does anyone here know what that story is? *(Response — Someone will surely come up with Jonah.)*

Yes, it's the story of a prophet named Jonah. Who can tell me what a prophet is? *(Responses — Preacher, one who tells the future, a wise man, a seer, and so forth.)* Yes, Jonah was chosen by God to be his spokesman. He was told to go to a wicked city called Nineveh to tell the people to repent and turn to God.

But Jonah decided he didn't want to do what God told him so he got in a ship to run away. Do you know what word we use that means not to do what we are told to do? *(Response — Someone will say disobedience.)*

Yes, and Jonah was disobedient. Are you ever disobedient? I suppose I could ask your parents about that, couldn't I?

Well, as disobedient Jonah was running away, a great storm came up and threatened the boat in which he was traveling.

It was decided after much debate that the sailors should throw Jonah out of the boat, and when they did the storm stopped. God prepared "a great fish" (we believe it must have been a whale) to swallow Jonah, and then when Jonah was sorry for his disobedience, the fish spit him out on dry land.

Wasn't that a terrifying ordeal to have to go through to learn to be obedient to God?

Hopefully, we won't have to be swallowed by a whale to learn that God wants us to be obedient to him. We can learn obedience by the little things we are required to do at home, so that when God speaks to us about what He wants us to do, we will obey.

This whale is a reminder for you of Jonah and how he learned to obey. *(Pass out stickers.)*

(Prayer to help us learn obedience.)

5

Thanks For Today

Psalm 118:24: This is the day that the Lord has made.

Object: A sheet of plain white paper

Good morning, boys and girls. Look what I've got with me today. *(Wait for reaction.)* What is this paper for? What are some of the uses we could make of it? *(Take four or five answers or suggest some.)* We could write a letter or story, draw a picture, roll it into a ball, tear it to bits, cut it into shapes, fold it, make an airplane.

Yes, I could do any of those things with my sheet of paper. Now let me tell you what I want to represent with this paper today. *(Read Psalm 118:24.)*

Let my paper represent the day that the Lord has given me today. If I were to represent my life, I would have one page for each day I have lived. Wouldn't that be a tall stack of paper?

In a very real sense, our days are like a sheet of paper. We record our deeds and actions of a lifetime in the volume that measures our lives. It is a book read by others as well as recorded with God.

We can make each day a day of praise and blessing, or a day of disobedience and badness — happiness, failure, or accomplishment. God has given us each day just as a clean, new sheet of paper, to do with as we will.

Will you think of your days as a gift from God to use in ways that bring joy to you, help to others, and praise to God?

I've decided to make my day a happy one. So, I'm going to ... *(Do something with your paper — like a paper airplane that is then sailed into the congregation.)*

(Prayer of thanks for today.)

6
Fishers Of Men

Matthew 4:19: Follow me ...
Mark 1:17: ... I will make you fishers of men.

Object: Fish stickers, erasers, or tiny toys (If you are a fisherman you might wear a favorite fishing hat.)

Good morning, boys and girls. How many of you children have ever been on a fishing trip? I've done that and it is really fun. Sometimes I let the fish go after I've caught them, 'cause it's the fun of the catch that I enjoy most. Although sometimes if I'm out camping I fry the fish and have a good meal.

There are lots of different kinds of fish one can catch. Can you name any that you have caught? *(Responses — Trout, bass, perch, and so forth.)* Sounds like good fish stories to me!

Do you know that there are people who are paid to fish? They do it for a living. They go out in big boats, far out into the oceans, to catch tons of fish. What do we call people who fish for a living? *(Response.)*

Yes, that's right. We call them fishermen, just the same as those who do it for sport.

Do you know that Jesus was friends with some fishermen? Can anybody name one of them? *(Responses — Andrew, Peter, James, John.)* They were fishermen on the Sea of Galilee. One day when Jesus met them He said, "Come, follow me, and I will make you fishers of men."

Wasn't that a strange thing to say? What do you suppose He meant by that? *(Response.)*

He meant that God is seeking men and women to be his people in a special relationship, and that He was going to use people to help bring others into his kingdom.

Jesus has extended that invitation to us as well. He will use us to be fishers of men.

Do you know how we can do that? *(Response.)*

We tell others what Jesus means to us, and how He loves them and died to forgive their sins, and we win them into God's kingdom.

Wouldn't you like to be *that* kind of fisherman? Okay, here is a little fish symbol to remind you that you can be one of Jesus' fishermen. *(Pass out fish symbols.)*

(Prayer to help us tell others of our faith.)

7

The Shepherd Cares For His Sheep

Psalm 100:3: The sheep of his pasture.
Isaiah 40:11: Like a shepherd, He will tend his flock.
Isaiah 53:6: All we like sheep have gone astray.
Luke 15:6: Found my sheep which was lost.
John 10:11: I am the good shepherd.
Hebrews 13:20: The great shepherd of the sheep.

Object: Lamb or sheep stickers

Good morning, boys and girls. Who can tell me where New Zealand *(Montana, Australia, Israel — any sheep-producing area)* is? *(Response. Help them with the location if it is remote or strange to them.)* I visited (place) for a period of time and saw lots and lots of sheep. Did you know that in New Zealand there are about 70 million sheep? That's about 20 or 25 sheep per person of the population.

Why do people raise sheep? *(Responses — Wool, meat, skins.)*

Sheep have to be looked after and taken care of. In some places they have to be moved great distances to find enough pasture for them to graze. Do you know what a person who tends the sheep is called? *(Response.)*

Yes, a shepherd. Many shepherds spend long days with their sheep, and can even tell them apart, although they all look alike to us sometimes.

The Bible tells us that we are like sheep, and that we need a shepherd to take care of us, to feed us, to find us when we get lost, and to keep us from going astray. Who is our shepherd? *(Responses — God, Jesus, even the pastor may be suggested.)*

We have lots of word pictures in the Bible that tell us of the special love that God has for us as part of his flock. He knows each one of us by name and is always searching for us to bring us into the safety of his fold.

Jesus said that his sheep heard his voice and came to him. As good sheep we need to be listening to hear the voice of our master.

(Prayer to help us to know the safety that comes from being in the care of the Great Shepherd.)

(Give each child a sheep sticker.)

8
Christ Comes Into Our Hearts

1 Samuel 16:7: The Lord looks at the heart.
1 Chronicles 28:9: Serve him with a whole heart.
Psalm 44:21: He knows the secrets of the heart.
Psalm 51:10: Create in me a clean heart.
Matthew 5:8: Blessed are the pure in heart.
Romans 10:10: With the heart, man believes.
Ephesians 3:17: May Christ dwell in your heart.

Object: Heart stickers

Good morning, boys and girls. *(Show heart symbol.)* What is this symbol? *(Response — heart.)* Why do you suppose we have made such a symbol of one of the inner organs of the body? What does it represent? *(Responses — Love, sweethearts, romance, and so forth.)*

When we talk about love, we are really talking about a feeling, aren't we? Part of that is intellectual, that is, what we think with our minds. But part of it seems to be deep down inside of us.

Do you really think love comes out of that muscle that is beating in your chest? Let's be quiet for a minute and feel our hearts. *(Hands on chest or on pulse.)* Do you feel it?

When you say you love someone — like your mother or father, or even your brother or sister — how do you feel? *(Responses — Something inside, excited, happy, and so forth.)*

Is it a different feeling inside than you usually have? Well, that's why God tells us that it is important what kind of secrets we have there in the deepest parts of our being. That's why the Bible says that it is with our hearts that we respond to God.

He loved us so much that He sent Jesus to be our Savior, and as we believe in our hearts, God brings an understanding of real love to us.

21

Let this little heart remind you to love God **and** your neighbor, because God loves you. *(Give each child a heart sticker.)* *(Prayer of response in love, to God.)*

9
Baptism/Dedication

(This message is most appropriate when children have been invited forward as participants to witness an act of baptism or dedication.)

Proverbs 22:6: Train up a child in the way he should go.
Mark 10:14: Let the children come to me.
Luke 2:22: They brought him to Jerusalem to present him to the Lord.
Acts 16:33: He was baptized and all his household.

Object: Plastic baby pins in pink and blue (Available as baby shower decorations in shops.)

Good morning, boys and girls. We have just been a part of a very happy and special occasion in the life of one of our families here in the church. We have been a part of a very spiritual experience for we have witnessed a family who has brought their child to God's House to dedicate themselves and the child to God. The parents have made a pledge to God that they will, with his help, raise their child to be a disciple of Jesus when the time comes for his/her own personal confession of faith. This is a very solemn and important decision for Christian parents to make.

Boys and girls, do you remember when your parents brought you to the church for your (baptism/dedication)? Probably not, because you were just a wee baby. Did you know that Jesus was only eight days old when his parents took him to the temple and dedicated him to God? You can read about that in the second chapter of Luke's gospel.

Well, what do you think it means to be dedicated to the Lord? *(Responses — You belong to God; you become a Christian; you will follow Jesus; you will love God. A great variety of answers will be given which may need clarification or may be the springboard for a teaching gem.)*

What we do here doesn't change a person or make him or her a Christian. What it does is identify that person with the people of God in a special way. We say that we want our children to grow to be believers in God and disciples of the Lord Jesus.

Let's all think of what it means to believe in God and be the disciples of the Lord Jesus.

(Prayer of blessing on children and remembrance of the promises made at the Baptism/Dedication.)

(Give out the pins to mark the happy event.)

10
Saint Valentine, Bishop Of Love

1 Chronicles 28:9: Serve him with a whole heart.
Psalm 19:14: Let the words of my mouth and the meditations of my heart ...
Psalm 119:11: Thy word have I hid in my heart.
Mark 12:30: Love the Lord ... with all your heart.

Object: Candy hearts (may need to be censored!)

Good morning, boys and girls. Do you know what a tradition is? *(Responses — may be interesting!)* A tradition is a story or a custom that is passed from generation to generation, usually without being written down. For example, your grandfather or great-grandfather might have always done something special at people's birthdays and the family adopted that practice and continued it, sometimes even forgetting where it started.

Well, there is a very old tradition about a Bishop named Valentinus who lived back in the days of the Roman Empire. It seems as though the Roman officials had a rule against young people being married in the church.

Many young Christians wanted to be married by the priest in the church with God's blessing. Valentinus was sympathetic to these people and continued to marry them even though he was often threatened by the government authorities. Finally he was taken to Rome and put to death for his faith and his defiance of the Emperor's rule.

In memory and honor of this man, young sweethearts started talking about choosing a Valentine when they were talking about choosing a bride.

Valentinus was later declared to be a saint by the Roman Catholic church and his name has come down to us in the day we call Saint Valentine's Day.

He served God with all his heart and the heart symbol is chosen to represent his day. We use the day and the symbol now to tell people how much we love them, don't we?

(Prayer that we learn to share love each day.)

(Pass out candy hearts.)

11
Saint Patrick, Missionary

Matthew 28:19: Go and make disciples.

Object: Shamrock stickers or pins (Perhaps a shamrock pin might be worn today.)

Good morning, boys and girls. Today I want to tell you an adventure story! It's about a young boy of sixteen who lived back around 300 A.D.

Some raiders came ashore in the land where he lived and captured him and took him away to their homeland across the sea where he was made a slave.

After about six years, he escaped and was able to find a ship to take him home again. He was happy to be back with his family.

Shortly after his return home God gave him a vision to return to the land where he had been a slave to tell them about Jesus. Wasn't that a brave thing to do?

He preached all over the country amidst much persecution, but won many converts to the Christian faith and founded a church in the land.

Now, from what I've told you, is there anyone here who can tell me the name of this brave, adventurous Christian missionary? *(Response — Saint Patrick.)* And what is the name of the country where he told the good news? *(Response — Ireland.)*

There are lots of fables and stories which have grown up around Patrick. It is interesting to learn the true facts about the man. He did not drive the snakes out of Ireland; he did not receive sainthood; he was not a Roman Catholic, and he is buried in the cemetery of the Protestant church in Dublin.

It is important for us to remember that he was a man who responded to God's call to be a missionary, and went back to the people who had mistreated him, to tell them about Jesus Christ. He was one of the early missionaries who wanted everyone to know the Good News of God's love.

(Prayer that we might see how God can use us to tell his story to others.)

(Give each child a shamrock in recognition of Saint Patrick's missionary work.)

12

Thinking About The Cross

Matthew 10:38: Take his cross and follow me.
Luke 9:23: Take up his cross daily, and follow me.
Luke 9:51: He resolutely set his face to Jerusalem.
Galatians 6:14: That I should never boast except in the cross of
Jesus Christ.

Object: Pocket crosses

Good morning, boys and girls. When we look back to the life
of Jesus, one of the first things that comes to mind is the cross! In
fact, the symbol of the cross is one of the most honored and
recognizable of Christianity. It has been fashioned in jewelry, it is
used to decorate churches and homes, and there are songs about it.
Why do you think the cross is so prominent in the church and in
the life of Jesus? *(Response — Because He died on the cross.)*

Do you know that the symbol of the cross that we like to see
was once a symbol of shame? It was a dreadful thing for anyone to
be hanged from a tree or nailed to a cross. It was a death penalty
that was only given to the worst of criminals. Was Jesus a criminal?
(Response — No, He was_____.)

Jesus died on the cross as part of God's plan for winning the
world back to himself.

Do you know that Jesus knew that He was going to die on a
cross? He told his friends that He was going to Jerusalem and that
evil men there would put him to death. He also told them that as
his followers they should be prepared to bear their own crosses.

During these days before Easter, we shall be talking and thinking
a lot about the cross because we know that in dying on the cross,
Jesus made it possible for each of us to be forgiven and made new
by God through his sacrifice.

Have you ever seen a pocket cross? *(Show one.)* I am going to
carry this little cross in my pocket as a reminder of God's love to

29

me. I'd like to invite you to join me. Would you like that? *(Pass out pocket crosses.)*

(Prayer: Thank you, God, for the symbol of the cross that reminds us of Jesus' love for you and your love for us.)

13
Triumphal Entry

Matthew 21:9: Hosanna to the Son of David.
Mark 11:9: Hosanna! Blessed is He who comes in the name of the Lord.
Luke 19:38: Blessed is the king who comes in the name of the Lord.
John 12:13: Took branches of the palm trees and went to meet him.

Object: Palm frond or leaf

Good morning, boys and girls. I love a parade! Don't you? How many of you have ever been in a parade? *(Response — Let a few share.)* At parades there is always such a joyful spirit. People are usually happy and there is lots of cheering and festivity.

Have you ever heard of a ticker-tape parade? Well, in New York City and in some other big cities in the world, when very famous or heroic persons are being welcomed to the city, they throw paper and streamers out of the high office windows to shower onto the parade below. It started as a very spontaneous act by some people who were very excited.

Did you know that Jesus once had a parade? He was going into Jerusalem for the Jewish Feast of Passover. When the people in the city who knew about him heard it, they decided to go out and meet him.

They were excited! They even wanted to make him their king! To show how much they honored him, they took off their coats and wraps and laid them down like a red carpet before him. They even tore branches off the palm trees and waved them in the air like flags to welcome him into the city.

That's why we call this day Palm Sunday. It was and is a day of rejoicing because the King is coming!

Would you like to have a parade today? Good! Take your palm branch and let's parade up and down the aisle of the church and shout, "Hosanna to the King. Hosanna to Jesus!" *(Do it! Ask the congregation to join in. It is a good idea to pass out palms on the way in this Palm Sunday instead of the traditional way out.)*

(After the parade — a prayer proclaiming Christ the King!)

14
He Is ALIVE!

Matthew 28:1-8: Jesus is risen!
Mark 16:1-13: Do not be amazed. He is risen. He is not here!
Luke 24:1-12: The stone was rolled away from the tomb.
John 20:1-18: Mary met the risen Lord.

Object: Angels, open tomb, or lily on cards or stickers

He is alive! He **is** alive! He is **alive**! That was the message of the angels who greeted Jesus' friends at the empty tomb on Easter morning! Can you imagine how shocked and surprised and excited and scared those people were when they saw angels and an empty grave?

After Jesus died on the cross and was buried in a borrowed tomb, all of his followers were sad and brokenhearted. Their friend and teacher had been taken away from them. And even though He had told them of his death and that He would rise from the dead, they had trouble believing that it really had happened.

Today there are jubilant people all aver the world who are crying out, "He is **alive**!" Over 600 million people who claim the name "Christian" are excited about the good news that Jesus is alive. But often, like the early followers, they don't really understand what that means.

I want you young people to try to understand what the story of Easter really means to you and me today.

If Jesus is really alive, as we believe He is, then He cares for us today. We can talk to him and know his presence with us no matter where we are or what we are doing. If He is alive, He is able to hear our prayers and send his Holy Spirit to us to confirm our faith. And most importantly, the Bible tells us that He can come to be alive in us.

There is a great Easter hymn that we sing titled "He Lives," and it ends with the words "You ask me how I know He lives, He

33

lives within my heart." I hope every one of us in this place this morning knows that He lives because we have invited him to live in our hearts.

(Prayer of rejoicing and praise for the living Savior, alive in the world both now and forever.)

(Give the children their Easter reminder.)

15
Forgiveness Of Sins

Psalm 51:1: Blot out sins.
Jeremiah 31:34: Remember no more.
1 John 1:7: Blood of Lamb cleanses us from all sin.

Object: Erasers or pencils with erasers

Good morning, boys and girls. Ever make a mistake? I've made a great many in my lifetime. What kind of mistakes have you made? *(Take four or five responses.)*

Well, today I want to talk about the kinds of mistakes we make when we are doing paperwork, like in school, on a test, or when you make a mistake writing a letter or drawing a picture. If you suddenly think of the answer to a question after you've already written in an answer, what can you do about that? *(Response — Someone will say erase it or rub it out.)*

When I was a small boy in school I didn't always have an eraser, so I would wet my finger and rub the paper. It made a terrible mess! Aren't you glad that someone invented erasers? Erasers make it possible for us to start over and correct our mistakes.

You know, God has a way in which He deals with our mistakes. Do you know what that is? *(Response — someone will mention Jesus.)* Yes, that's it. He forgives us when we confess our sins and failures, and He makes things clean and new in our lives. In fact, the Bible says He blots out our sins. He remembers them no more because the Blood of Jesus cleanses us from all our sins.

I'm going to give you this eraser to remind you of this story — but remember, though an eraser may leave a bit of a smudge behind, the cleansing which God applies to our sins leaves us wholly clean and makes us just like new again. *(Give the children the erasers.)*

(Prayer of thanks for God's cleansing.)

16
Careful With Those Lips

Psalm 119:171: Lips utter praise.
Psalm 141:3: Set a guard on my mouth — watch the door of my lips.
Isaiah 6:5: Man of unclean lips — people of unclean lips.
Matthew 15:8: Honor with lips.
Romans 3:13: Poison on lips.
1 Peter 3:10: Refrain lips from evil.

Object: Lips stickers

Good morning, boys and girls. I'm thinking of an external part of the human body that you use all the time, whether you are walking, standing still, sitting down, awake or asleep. Can anyone guess which part of the body I have in mind? *(Responses — Allow eight or ten. If they have not said mouth or lips, you can give them a couple of clues.)* I'm using them right now. Eyes? No. *(Purse your lips.)*

That's right. I'm thinking about lips today. Well, what a strange thing that is to think about. Is it? Lips are very useful. Why don't you tell me about some ways in which you use yours. *(Responses — whistle, taste, eat, pucker, kiss, talk, pout.)*

Do you know that the Bible has lots of things to say about lips? It talks about how we use our lips for good and evil. Can you think of some ways we might use our lips that would be evil? *(Responses — swear, lie, make ugly faces, tattle, and so forth.)*

Now, how about naming some of the ways in which we use our lips for good. *(Responses — sing, praise God, tell the truth, speak kindly, kiss a loved one, share good news, and so forth.)*

Yes, the Bible says we can use our lips to curse or to praise God. It is one of the marks of a disciple of Jesus that he or she uses his/her lips to bring praise to God. *(Pass out stickers.)*

May these lips remind you how to use yours properly.

(Prayer of help to use our lips to God's glory.)

17
The Shepherd King

Psalm 23: The Lord is my shepherd.

Object: Bookmarks with Psalm 23

Good morning, boys and girls. In Israel there is a place between Jerusalem and Jericho called the Valley of Shadows. It is a deep ravine that has been cut out of the countryside by the waters which cascade down from the hill country on their way to the River Jordan.

Shepherds may often be seen in the fields above the Valley of Shadows as they tend their sheep and play on their flutes, like David did in that place when he was a boy.

What can you tell me about David? *(Responses — He was a shepherd, he killed Goliath, he became king of Israel, he wrote the psalms. [The psalms is the one you are looking for.])*

Yes, one of the things that David did was to write songs. Have you ever sung or read one of David's songs? *(Response — They may not know that Psalms is a songbook. It would be helpful to have a Bible handy to turn to and leaf through the book of Psalms.)*

In his songs, David sang praises to God. He sang about God's creation, God's love, God's majesty, and about how God took care of him. We do that same thing in some of the hymns and songs we sing today, don't we?

One of the best known of David's songs is one that I believe he wrote while he was on that hillside as a young boy on Israel. Do you know which one I'm thinking of? *(Response — Psalm 23.)* Does anyone know how it starts? Well, I've got some bookmarks here with it printed on them. I'm going to give one to each of you so that we may all say it together. *(There will be enough who can read to help carry it and some of the younger ones may know part of it. Recite together.)*

(Prayer: We thank God for David, who taught us how to sing praises to God.)

18

Jesus And The Ten Commandments

Exodus 20:1-18: The Ten Commandments.
Deuteronomy 5:6-21: Ten Commandments.
Deuteronomy 11:8, 9: Keep every commandment.
Matthew 22:36-40: Which is the greatest commandment?
Romans 13:10: Love, fulfillment of the Law.
Galatians 3:24: The Law has become our schoolmaster.

Object: Bookmarks or cards with Ten Commandments

Good morning, boys and girls. In the Old Testament book of Exodus, and repeated in Deuteronomy, there is the story of the tablets of stone that Moses received from God when he went up onto Mount Sinai. Can anyone here tell me what we call the words written on those stone tablets? *(Response.)* Yes, they have come to be known as the Ten Commandments. How many of you have learned something about the Ten Commandments? *(Hands.)* Okay, now which of you can tell me what the Commandments say? *(Responses — You may get them all or most of them. You may even have some children who can say them all.)*

Why do you suppose God gave his people these Commandments? *(Responses — To tell them how to behave; so they might learn to be good; to regulate society; to teach them, and so forth. You want to get to a basic standard of relationship between God and man, and man to man.)*

God expects humankind to respond to him and to each other in ways which will honor him. The Ten Commandments have long been the standard by which we measure how well we are doing in these relationships.

Lots of times people have tried to ignore these and other laws that God has given. Often this is because they don't want to do what God has told them to do. They try to excuse their behavior. Do you know what it means to try to excuse the way you act?

(Response — Encourage examples from the children of what that means.)

When Jesus was on earth, people questioned him on which one of the Commandments He thought was the most important. Do you know what He said? *(Read Matthew 22:36.)*

Jesus said that the fulfillment of all the law and the teachings of the prophets in the Old Testament depends upon LOVE, love for God and love for our neighbors. It is important, boys and girls, that we learn how to really love God and one another. The Bible is our guide and the Holy Spirit is our teacher. Won't you ask God to help you each day to learn how to love?

(Prayer to ask God for help in learning to love.)

(Give them Ten Commandment bookmarks or cards.)

19

Her Children Bless Her

Exodus 20:12: Honor your father and mother.
Proverbs 31:28: Her children rise up and bless her.

Object: Carnations

Good morning, boys and girls. Today is a special day, isn't it? It's not a holiday as such, but it is a day that we set aside to honor our mothers. It is right for us to do that because we have been instructed in the Bible to do so. But, more than that, mothers are sort of special people to us, aren't they?

Would you like to know how we have come to have a Mother's Day? It's not just a day devised by card companies, florists, and candy makers to sell their products. Actually, a day for honoring mothers was observed many years ago in England and it was called "Mothering Sunday" and came in mid-Lent. Then, in 1907, under the inspiration of Miss Anna M. Jarvis of Graftoll, West Virginia, and later Philadelphia, a day was arranged for sons and daughters to pay tribute to their mothers. She arranged a special service in her church and asked everyone to wear white carnations. The plan was so appealing that by 1911 it had spread all over the country and in 1914 was officially designated as "Mother's Day" by Congress. The custom then became the wearing of a white carnation by those whose mothers had passed on and a red carnation by those whose mothers were still living. That's the beautiful custom that I grew up with and which many people still observe.

And so to all our Moms today, we say, "We love you for being special people in our lives." We are going to hold hands and say a prayer. Then I want each of you to give your mom a flower, and if she's not here you can take it home to her or give it to someone else.

(Prayer of thanksgiving for mothers. Give them the carnations.)

20
The Golden Rule

Matthew 7:12: Whatever you want others to do for you.
Galatians 6:7: Whatever a man sows, that he shali also reap.

Object: Rulers, 6 inch, with Golden Rule imprint

Good morning, boys and girls. Do you recognize what I have with me today? *(Response.)* Yes, it's something very common. You all probably have one in your desk at school or in your room at home. A ruler is a very useful object, isn't it? What are some of the things one might use it for? *(Responses — measure height, width, length, mark off a graph, help draw straight lines, and so forth.)*

Yes, those are all good uses. I think one of the most important things about a ruler is that it sets a standard for us. If our ruler is marked off in inches or centimeters, provided it has been marked off properly by the manufacturer, we can always depend on it to give us the proper measurement if we use it correctly. If that weren't true, then we could never build anything. We are dependent upon having a sure standard.

We Christians have a standard by which we may measure our lives before God. Can anyone think of what that standard is? *(Response — the Bible.)* Yes, the Bible is our standard. We measure ourselves by what God has taught us in his book.

There is a verse in the Bible that has come to be known as "The Golden Rule." Does anyone know what it says? *(Response — someone will get it right.)* That's it! What does that mean to you? *(Responses — Varied and personal. May either require comment or be complete in themselves.)*

Well, let's remember that Golden Rule as we go through the day today and seek to make it a standard rule in our lives.

I have here a Golden Rule reminder for each of you. *(Pass out the rulers.)*

(Prayer to incorporate the truth into our lives each day.)

41

21
Birthday Of The Church

Acts 2:1-4: Filled with the Holy Spirit.

Object: Balloons or birthday candles

Good morning, boys and girls. Does anyone here have a birthday this week (this month)? *(Responses.)* Are you excited about it? Will you have a party? Do you know who will be at your party? Do you know what presents you will get? Parties are fun, aren't they?

Do you know what I think is part of the great fun of parties and special events? It is the anticipation. Your imagination is filled with all the possibilities of joy. You get excited and more excited as the event draws closer and closer. Sometimes you feel like you **just can't wait!**

The disciples of Jesus had an experience like that. Before Jesus went back to be with God, He told them to wait in Jerusalem because God was going to release his power on them.

That day was called "Pentecost" and, after the anticipation and excitement of waiting, God did just as Jesus had promised. He released his mighty power on those disciples. And they preached and spoke to people from all over the world who were in Jerusalem in their native tongues, and thousands of people believed in Jesus.

Pentecost became the birthday of the church! That's why we celebrate today, because since that day God has been doing new and wonderful things by the power of his Holy Spirit in the world.

I think a birthday celebration calls for balloons (candles), don't you? Let's celebrate what God is doing in his church today and through his Holy Spirit.

(Prayer that God will fill his church today with the power of his Holy Spirit.)

(Give out balloons. If possible, inflated are preferable, but just the uninflated are sufficient.)

42

22
The Value Of A Smile

Proverbs 16:20: Happy is he who trusts in the Lord.
John 15:11: That my joy might be in you.
Galatians 5:22: The fruit of the Spirit is love, joy ...

Object: Smiley face stickers or pins (It would be helpful to have a large yellow "Happy Face" visual aid prepared beforehand.)

Good morning, boys and girls. *(Show "Happy Face.")* Does everybody here know what we call this symbol that we now see everywhere these days? *(Response — A happy face.)* And do you know what happens to this happy face if I turn it upside down? It becomes a grumpy face, doesn't it? *(Demonstrate.)*

Let's see how many of you can make a really happy face today. *(Have them face the congregation.)* Now let's see your grumpiest face. Oh, that's awful! Please turn around so the people don't have to look at you.

Now, I have a question for you. Which face was the easiest for you to make? *(Responses should be overwhelming for the happy face. This might open up an opportunity for talking about attitudes which are reflected on our faces.)*

People who study things like the functions of the body have actually discovered that it takes fewer muscles to smile than it does to frown. Did you know that?

When we are happy and have a smile on our faces we tend to make other people who are around us happy as well. The same thing is true when we have sad or grumpy faces. Isn't it surprising how we can have an influence on other people just because of the look on our faces?

I think God wants Christian people to be attractive so that others will see the happiness of their lives expressed on their faces and want to know how they find happiness in their lives.

Do you think you can remember to keep your happy face on this week? Maybe this little sticker I have for you will remind you. *(Pass out the stickers.)*

(Prayer for happy hearts and the joy of the Lord.)

23
The Call To Follow

Matthew 4:19: He said, "Come, follow me."
Matthew 16:24: Take up his cross and follow me.
Luke 22:39: ... and the disciples followed him.
John 21:22: You, follow me.

Object: Apostles' bookmarks or cards

Good morning, boys and girls. Do you know the names of the twelve men who were Jesus' closest friends? Do you know what they were called? *(Response.)* Yes, we call them the Twelve Apostles! Do you know what the work "apostle" means? *(Responses — Some guesses may be close; allow some expression.)*

An apostle is a learner. It may also mean "a messenger." So the Twelve Apostles were persons who learned and were sent out with a message. What was the message that they were to tell? *(Responses — About God, about Jesus, and so forth.)* The apostles went out to tell people the truths that they were learning from their teacher. And who was their teacher? *(Response — Jesus.)* Yes, Jesus spent a lot of his time alone with these twelve friends, teaching them about his father, God, and of all the things that God wanted people to know about him. He taught them what the scriptures of the old Testament meant. Most of all, He showed his love to them and to others with whom He came into contact. He taught them a great deal about what love means.

After Jesus died on the cross, was buried, rose again, and went back to God, his learner/messengers went all over the country and even into many foreign countries to tell people what they had learned.

I'm going to give you each a card with the apostles' names on it and ask you to say them out loud with me. *(After giving the cards, have the children stand and face the congregation as they read the names together.)*

Thank you, boys and girls, for helping us remember the names of those twelve friends of Jesus.

Does what they did give you any ideas about what we ought to be doing? *(Response — Learning about God and Jesus from the Bible and then going out to tell others about him.)*

(Prayer that we might be disciples who learn the truth and share it with others.)

24
The Love Of God

John 3:16: For God so loved the world.
John 15:13: Greater love has no man than this.
Ephesians 5:2: Walk in love, just as Christ loved you.

Object: "Jesus loves me" stickers, buttons, balloons, and so forth

Good morning, boys and girls. I want you to help me sing a song today. It is one of the first songs I ever learned, and it is a song that I believe everybody in this congregation knows. Do you know what song we're going to sing together? *(Responses — Many may be good and/or familiar, but when you get "Jesus Loves Me"...)* That's the one! *(Sing the song together.)*

Do you know that we rarely sing that song in a church worship service? Because it's a simple little song known by everyone and sung by children in Sunday School, I guess we have come to think of ourselves as too sophisticated or grown up to sing a little song like that. But I like it!

Do you know why I like that song so much? *(Response.)* There are many reasons to like the song "Jesus Loves Me," but the reason I like it so well is because of the story it tells me.

I need to be reminded all the time that Jesus loves me, and of where I can go to read about how much He does. Where do you learn about how much Jesus loves me? *(Response — Bible.)*

Do you read about how much He loves you? Do you think we could get all the people, old and young, big and small, to join us in singing the song one more time? *(All congregation sings.)*

(Give out "Jesus Loves Me" memento.)

(Prayer: Lord, help us to know that you love us, even those times that we feel most unlovely.)

25

The Order Of The Universe

Exodus 13:21: Cloud by day to lead.
Psalm 119:105: ...a light to my path.
Proverbs 16:9: The Lord directs his steps.
Matthew 3:3: Make his paths straight.

Object: Magnetic compasses

Good morning, boys and girls. Boys and girls, I have an instrument in my hand which will always tell me the same truth no matter where I am on the earth. Can anybody guess what it is? *(Response — Someone should get it.)*

This is a magnetic compass. It will always point to magnetic north, even if I am away down in South America, or Australia, or New Zealand. I might be on a ship or on land or in an airplane, and still the little needle in here will always point to magnetic north.

Well, of what use is a little instrument like this? *(Responses.)* Boy Scouts, Girl Scouts, and campers know what it is good for, don't they? It helps you to locate yourself and keep from getting lost. It can help you find which way to go. That's very useful.

I know of another item that is very useful when you are trying to find out which way you should go. Do you know what I have in mind? *(Responses may be interesting.)*

In Psalm 119:105 we read, "Your Word is a lamp to me and a light to my path."

In a very real way, the Bible is like a compass. If we are confused and wonder which way we should go in life, or what our behavior should be, we can go to the Bible and receive direction. It helps us to find the right path to walk.

This little compass is just a toy and may not work as well as a regular one, but it will remind you that God has given us a guide to help us find our way. *(Pass out compasses.)*

(Prayer for openness to follow in his pathway.)

48

26
Captives Set Free

John 8:32: The truth shall make you free.
Galatians 5:1: Christ has set us free.

Object: Keys

Good morning, boys and girls. *(Hold up a key ring with various keys, or provide some different and interesting looking keys.)* Aren't keys fun? Do you like keys? How many of you have your own keys? And what are your keys for? *(Responses.)* Keys are very useful things, except when they get lost. Without keys we sometimes find it impossible to carry on. What kind of a key would you say is a most important one? *(Responses — car, house.)*

Do you know that there are lots of people in the world who are in prisons? They are not free. Sometimes they are locked up because they have broken the law and are being punished, but sometimes they are locked in prison because of their beliefs. They believe in a different form of government, or they believe that all people have the right to be free and they are being denied their own freedom. Some of Jesus' followers were thrown into prison for preaching and teaching about him. He was even thrown into prison and condemned just before his death.

Jesus talked about a key that would set men free. Do you know what kind of a key He meant? *(Response — Someone will probably say "truth." If not, introduce it.)*

Jesus said, "The truth will make you free." He also said, "I am the way, the truth, and the life. No man comes to the Father but by me." In that, He meant that He is the truth that can set us free from sin and allow us to come to God.

This is a most important key. Of all the keys that we might have and use in our lifetimes, it is more important than all the rest, for it opens heaven for us and brings us into the presence of God.

(Prayer for spiritual freedom and knowledge of the truth that is Jesus Christ. Give out keys as a symbol of our freedom in Christ.)

27

I Love A Parade

Psalm 33:12: Blessed is the nation whose God is the Lord.

Object: Matchstick flags or flag stickers

Good morning, boys and girls. I love a parade, don't you? It is always exciting to see the marching bands, the banners, the floats and flags, and all the happy spectators. There is something festive and happy about a parade. It seems like a great big party that moves down the road or avenue. In America we have lots of parades for lots of different occasions, don't we? Have you ever been in a parade? *(Responses — Allow a few brief ones.)*

This is a particular time of year that we celebrate with parades, isn't it? The Fourth of July is a special day for us. Do you know why? *(Response — You are looking for Independence Day.)*

Yes! I think it is always important for us to know what we are celebrating. I suppose you could have a parade without any reason and not celebrate anything. At the Disney centers they have a parade every night just for the fun of it, perhaps to celebrate the happy mood of the people who are there, and that's okay too!

But when we celebrate our national Independence Day, it's good for us to remember what it means.

Our nation was founded on principles of liberty, justice, and the rights of people. One of those rights was the freedom to worship God by the dictates of our conscience. That means that as we gather to worship God today in this place, we do so without fear or worry because our government protects our right to do so. We are very privileged in America to be able to praise God for his blessings to us as a nation, and we need always to pray that our nation will be faithful to its pledge of honoring God by placing its trust in him.

I'll give you a little flag now, and you can have a parade as you go back to your seats *(or off to Sunday school, and so forth).*

(Prayer for the nation.)

28
Music Is For Praise

Psalm 33:3: Sing to the Lord a new song.
Psalm 100:2: Come before Him with joyful singing,
Ephesians 5:19: Hymns and spiritual songs.
Colossians 3:16: Singing with thankfulness.

Object: Note stickers

Good morning, boys and girls. How many of you like to sing? What is your favorite song? *(Response — Give time for some enthusiastic responses.)* If we allowed everybody here today to tell us what their favorite song is, I expect that there would be almost as many favorites as there are people here. Why do you suppose we have favorite songs? *(Responses will be varied.)* Yes, because they have very special meaning to us, or because they remind us of a very special event in our life, or sometimes for the simple reason that we like the tune.

All through the Bible we have stories of people singing, and we sing here in church whenever we meet for worship, don't we? What do we call the songs that we sing in church? *(Responses — Hymns, Psalms, Choruses, Anthems, and so forth.)* And why do you suppose that music is such an important part of our lives together? *(Responses — Because it makes us happy; because it is a gift from God, and so forth.)* Most of our songs in church are songs of praise. Singing songs is one of the ways we tell God what we feel about him and how happy we are to be his people. In olden days people were encouraged to sing of their love for God and in the New Testament the apostle Paul encouraged the people in early Christian gatherings to sing psalms, and hymns, and spiritual songs, and to make melody in their hearts. There is a wise old saying, "Music gladdens the heart."

Sometimes when we feel sad or lonely, or even frightened, singing a song will help to lift our spirits and make us feel good again. Let's thank God for all the varieties of music that He gives us to fill our lives with happiness.

(Prayer of thanks for the human expressions of joy and praise that we have through music. Hand out notes for "joy of music.")

29
Trust In God

Psalm 40:4: Blessed is the man who has made the Lord his trust.
Proverbs 28:25: He who trusts in the Lord will prosper.

Object: U.S. pennies

Good morning, boys and girls. Every piece of American money has a motto on it. Do you know what a motto is? *(Response.)* A motto is an inscription or saying that expresses the feeling of the group or individual. It is sort of the phrase which best describes the group or person. What kind of a motto would you have for yourself? *(Responses — Suggest a few like "Always Late," "Honesty and Truth," "I'll do it later," and so forth.)* Well, a long time ago the leaders of our country decided that our nation ought to have a motto. Do you know what that motto is? *(Response — Someone will surely get it, "In God We Trust.")*

We want to help everyone remember that motto because we have put it on the smallest coin and the largest sized note we print at the U.S. Mint.

Now, it's all right to have a motto, but it is more important that we know what the motto means. What do you think our national motto, "In God We Trust," means? *(Responses — Go with these where you can.)* Very basically, boys and girls, it means that as a nation we are confident that God will support and sustain us in the principles of justice and freedom in which we believe.

Some find it very curious that we print the motto on money because they think that we often trust more in money than we do in God. And maybe there have been times in our history when we put more trust in our weapons than we did in God.

Well, I, for one, am glad to have a reminder on every penny, because I think it is important for us as a nation to remember what we are saying about ourselves, and we ought to really live as a people who **do** trust God, in every area of our lives.

This new penny will remind you of our national motto. *(Pass out pennies.)*

(Prayer that our national trust might be in God.)

30
The Wise Use Of Time

Ecclesiastes 3: There is an appointed time for everything.

Object: Plastic toy watches

Good morning, boys and girls. How many of you can tell time? Well, most of you can, and some of you younger ones are learning by looking at clocks and watching *Sesame Street*, aren't you? How many of you have a watch? Hold them up for me! My, there are so many different kinds and colors.

Why do you suppose we need to tell time anyway? *(Responses — Varied; some may be quite useable in developing your theme.)*

We are people who are very oriented to time, aren't we? We need to know what time it is to get to school, to watch our favorite TV programs, to arrive at the dentist's for an appointment, to meet trains and buses and airplanes. Time is important to sports competitors who are trying to better their skills, or to students who have tests to finish in the time the teacher has allowed. Time is important to airlines and businesses so that they may operate on a regular schedule. Time is important to people who work because they are often paid by the length of time spent on their jobs. Time is an important way in which we arrange the activities and appointments in our lives.

What do you suppose would happen if we did away with all clocks? *(Response — Chaos.)*

I think one of the most important lessons that I have ever learned about time is that we should never waste it. Time is a gift from God and the Bible tells us that God has appointed times for all the important things in our lives. He has even appointed times for us to spend with him.

We should be wise about the way we use our time so that we please God while we are enjoying the precious gifts that He has given us.

I can't give you the gift of time, but I can give you this toy watch to remind you of time.

(Prayer that God will fill our times with his presence.)

31
Vine And Branches

John 15:1-11: I am the vine, you are the branches.
Galatians 5:22-23: The fruit of the Spirit.

Object: Fresh red or purple grapes or stickers

Good morning, boys and girls. While I was living in New Zealand, I was provided a home for the length of my stay that had beautiful gardens around it. I was asked to care for the gardens by the home owner. Beside the garage there was a nice grapevine. Since it was springtime, the fruit was beginning to form on the vine. As I had little experience with growing grapes in the past, I had to be instructed in how to tend the vines. *(The locale and the experience may be varied to fit your experience.)*

I saw lots of new little shoots along the vine and a couple of long new growth areas. I was surprised to be told that I needed to cut or pull these new pieces of growth off the vine. If that weren't done, the tiny grapes that were forming would be robbed of much of the nutrients they needed to be good full fruit at the time of harvest. It was hard for me to cut off all those little branches which were not going to bear fruit, but while I was doing it, I remembered a story that Jesus told about vines and branches.

He said that He was the true vine and He talked to his disciples about being branches that were supposed to be bearing fruit. What do you suppose Jesus had in mind when He told the disciples that they were to bear fruit? *(Response — Let the children express what it might mean to them.)*

The Bible tells us what the fruits of a Christian's life are to be. *(Galatians 5:22-23 may be read here.)* And these are the kinds of things that God wants to see in us.

Do you know how we are able to produce these good fruits? *(Responses — By being obedient, by reading our Bibles, by learning more about Jesus, and so forth.)* Well, in his story about the vine and branches, Jesus said that a branch has to stay firmly attached to the vine in order to bear fruit. I think this means that we have to stay attached to Jesus, to draw our life strength from him so that his life will flow through us and produce the good fruit of God in our lives.

(Prayer: Help us to learn and understand that our nourishment and strength in life come to us through Jesus.)

This piece of good fruit (or fruit sticker) will help you to remember about the vine and branches.

32
Our Constant Companion

Hebrews 13:5: I will never leave you or forsake you.

Object: Cards with "Footprints" poem

Good morning, boys and girls. How many of you have been walking on the beach recently? I went for a walk on the beach yesterday in the soft sand. That's a lot of fun, isn't it? You can make some great patterns in the sand with your feet, can't you? I once wrote my whole name out in the sand in tiny steps. You can see where others have walked, you can find animal tracks, and you can even use your footprints to find your way back if you go into the new areas where you haven't been before.

I want to read a poem to you this morning that teaches us a good lesson about Jesus. The author of the poem is unknown. The poem is called "Footprints." *(Read poem.)*

What does that poem teach us about Jesus? *(Responses — mostly it should evoke the response that Jesus is always with us.)*

The Bible says of Jesus in Hebrews, "He will never leave us or forsake us." And it says, "The Lord is my helper; I will never be afraid."

We ought to take confidence from the story of "Footprints" to know that even when we feel as though we are alone, Jesus is always there to help us through the bad times of life.

(Give copy of poem.)

(Prayer of thanksgiving to God for the supporting arms of Jesus.)

33

The Great Commission

Matthew 28:19: Go, therefore, and make disciples of all nations.
Mark 16:15: Go into all the world and preach the gospel.

Object: Map of the world or globe stickers (You will need a globe to refer to.)

Good morning, boys and girls. How many of you like to study geography? And how many of you have a globe at home like this one? Or maybe you have one in your classroom at school. I think globes are great fun. They are even more fun than maps because you can turn them over and see the bottom of the world or see how shape comes into the study of relationships between continents and countries. Even as a child, when I studied the globe I wanted to go right around the world and visit as many parts of it as I could. Have you ever felt like that? When I look at this globe, I see great big patches of it that I have never explored. I don't know how the people live, or what the countryside looks like in so many places. Though I've been here and here and here and even here *(indicate)*, I still have so much of the world that I've yet to see. Can any of you point to places out of this country to which you have been? *(Responses — Allow several to indicate places. Respond positively to their adventures.)*

Do you know that Jesus talked about this world with his disciples? He was concerned that God's love should reach every person on earth, even though He knew that He could never get to travel there and tell them the good news of his Father himself. So, he told his disciples to go into all the world and tell people about God. That process is still going on and there are still a few places where that message has not reached. Have you ever thought that maybe God would use you to become one of those people who goes to a land far away to teach them about God's love in Jesus Christ?

60

God continues to call people to that task. Sometimes we call them missionaries; sometimes they are just tourists or business people who share God's good news with others as they travel. We can all share God's good news with other people, can't we? I hope you will learn to do that.

(Give globe stickers.)

(Prayer: God, let us be about the business of sharing our faith to Jesus with all of the world as He told us to.)

34

The Lost And Found

John 10:14: I am the Good Shepherd. I know my sheep.

Object: Shepherd's crook or picture

Good morning, boys and girls. Have you ever been to a lost and found department? They have them in airports, bus depots, large department stores, and even in churches, because people often lose things when they are away from home. Sometimes we even lose things around home, don't we? I had a friend once who was always losing his glasses, sometimes when they were right on top of his head!

Have you ever lost anything? *(Responses — Allow a representative feedback.)* And what did you do when you lost it? *(Responses — Cry, tell someone, search, and so forth.)* Yes, we search hard for things that become lost, and we search all the harder in proportion to the value of the thing that we've lost. That's why it is always good to know about the lost and found department.

Shepherds are people who take care of sheep. Often they live lonely lives away up in the high pasture country where they are alone with their sheep. Shepherds sometimes lose things, too. Who can tell me what a shepherd is liable to lose? Yes, shepherds lose sheep, because sometimes they wander off from the flock or get themselves stranded in places where they can't get out.

Jesus told a story about a shepherd who had one hundred sheep. One got lost. The shepherd cared so much for that one sheep that he left the 99 who were safe and searched high and low for the lost one until he found it. Jesus used that story to tell us that God is like that when we get ourselves lost or stray away from God. He comes looking for us because He loves us as a part of his family and never wants to lose us.

The Bible says, "He (Jesus) came to seek and to save that which was lost." Aren't you glad that God sent Jesus into the world to find us?

(Prayer of thanksgiving for the Shepherd/Savior we have in Jesus.)

35

Troubles Into Opportunities

Matthew 13:45, 46: The pearl of great price.

Object: Imitation pearls

Good morning, boys and girls. *(Display a string of pearls. Have on hand an oyster shell if available.)* Do you know what we call this piece of jewelry that I hold in my hand this morning? *(Response — A string of pearls.)* That's right! Do you know what a pearl is? It is a gem that is taken out of the sea.

Jesus told a parable once in which He said that the Kingdom of God is like a merchant seeking fine pearls, who, upon finding one of great value, sold all he had so that he could buy it. In several places in the Bible pearls are listed with silver, gold, and precious stones.

Why do you suppose pearls are so valuable? *(Responses — Allow some speculation. May be able to pick up on answers.)* It is because very good pearls are so hard to find in the deep parts of the ocean.

Do you know where pearls come from in the oceans? They come from inside oysters. *(Display oyster shell if you have one.)* Isn't that a strange place to find a precious jewel? Well, how do you suppose they get inside an oyster shell? *(Response — let the children have a go at this one.)*

When a little piece of sand gets inside the oyster's shell and it can't get out, it hurts or irritates the oyster. Have you ever had a little stone in your shoe that caused your foot to hurt until you got it out? Well, the oyster deals with the problem by rolling the bit of sand up in a special fluid that it produces. That takes the sharp edge off the sand and makes the oyster more comfortable. As long as the foreign object remains, the oyster adds substance to the smooth little object inside. When we open the oyster and take that little coated piece of sand out, we call it a pearl.

Sometimes the things that come into our lives as irritations can be dealt with in ways that change them into wonderful moments in our lives. We can often make a few pearls of our own. It takes patience and prayer to do that.

(Prayer to learn how patience can turn bad situations into life's pearls.)

(Give them an imitation plastic pearl.)

36
Labor Day

Proverbs 14:23: In all labor there is a profit.
Luke 10:7: The laborer is worthy of his hire.

Object: Toy tools

Good morning, boys and girls. This is Labor Day Weekend in America. Does anybody know why we have this holiday, aside from it being the last weekend before many students go back to school? *(Responses — Someone will identify it as a time to recognize workers.)*

How big a list do you suppose we could make if we started to name all of the workers we can think of? There would be all the types of work that are represented by our parents and relatives, and a lot that we can think of in our communities. Let's name a few. *(Responses — You may want to have a pad and pencil and write down some as they are given.)*

My, that is a long list, isn't it? And we have not really gotten started on it yet. When we think of all the people who have to labor to keep us housed and fed and protected, it adds up to hundreds and hundreds of people. Many of them are unseen and go unnoticed. Many people have very menial jobs to do. But everyone helps contribute to make our society function.

Even on the days that we take off to celebrate, there have to be people on duty to see that our services continue.

It is amazing that God has given us the ability to build a world like we have. Along with that creative ability, however, He has given us some responsibilities. We have to learn also how to take care of the ecology of our planet so that future generations can also enjoy the blessings God has given us.

I suppose that means that many new types of labor with new kinds of jobs will come along in the future and we'll have even more people to recognize for their service to mankind.

Enjoy your holiday, but remember the people that we honor in our celebration. *(Give object.)*

(Prayer for all those who labor that society might continue to function.)

37

Back To School

Proverbs 22:6: Train up a child in the way he should go.

Object: Toy blackboards (craft shop)

Good morning, boys and girls. Raise hands, all of you who can't wait to get back to school! I knew there would be some of you who wouldn't be too eager about it! How do you suppose I knew that?

I remember that as a child I never wanted the summer vacation to end. I wanted to be free to play and have fun going on trips or off to my grandparents' house for a visit.

But, school starts again and we are soon involved in all the activities and the learning that goes on there, aren't we?

Why do you suppose it is so important for you to go to school, anyway? *(Responses — Some might be quite helpful and incorporated into your theme and may give a youthful perspective to education.)* Education is very important to us so that we can have leaders in future generations. Government, industry, the arts and sciences, commercial business, and even the church rely on the learning that goes on among children who are in school today.

I expect that some of you know what you would like to be when you become adults, don't you? Who would like to share your goal with us? *(Responses — Allow as many as you have time for.)* Maybe some of you are too young just now to know, but over the years you will be making decisions about your lives, and the learning that you are doing now will be very important to you one day. The Bible says, "Study to show yourselves approved unto God," and that applies not only to the study of the Bible that you do, but all study that you do that helps to prepare you to be all that God wants you to be.

We should be thankful for our educational system and for all the dedicated teachers who help us to learn about ourselves and our world. *(Give out blackboards.)*

(Prayer for students, schools, and teachers.)

38
The Name Jesus

Job: 1:21: Blessed be the name of the Lord.
Matthew 1:21: You shall call his name Jesus.
Acts 4:12: No other name under heaven.
Philippians 2:9: Name which is above every name.

Object: Cards — Sallman's *Head of Christ* (various backs available)

Good morning, boys and girls. Do you know how you got your name? *(Responses — Picked by relative; named after someone; somebody liked it; and so forth.)* How many of you picked your own names? Nobody? How many of you like your names? *(Don't press it!)* Names say a lot about people. Often names are chosen by parents because of their meanings. Does anyone here know the meaning of his or her name? *(Allow two or three if they want to respond. Tell meaning of your own name if you know it.)* Names may not be as important to us as they once were, but it is nice to have a name, isn't it?

When Jesus was born, somebody very special chose his name and sent a messenger to tell Joseph. Do you know who chose the name "Jesus" for the baby born in the manger? *(Response.)* God sent an angel to Joseph in a dream and told him to name the baby "Jesus." Do you know why God chose that name? *(Responses.)*

The name "Jesus" in the Hebrew language is Joshua and it means "Savior." God said, "It is He who will save his people from their sins."

We give a very special place to the name of Jesus in our worship and in our lives. We honor his name and know that it is a name that is above every other name because Jesus is the Son of God.

One of the most familiar pictures of Jesus that has ever been painted is by a man named Sallman. We don't really know what Jesus looked like because there were no cameras in those days and no one that we know of ever painted a portrait of him. But this little card will be a reminder for you of the man we know as our Lord. His name is Jesus. *(Give picture cards.)*

(Prayer to exalt and magnify the name of Jesus.)

39

The Drawing Power Of Christ

John 12:32: "If I be lifted up I will draw all men unto me."

Object: Toy magnet (Note: Be prepared with a magnet and several objects that will be attracted to it. Little metal figures would be very helpful!)

Good morning, boys and girls. How many of you have ever experimented with a magnet? Do you know what a magnet does? *(Responses.)* Do you understand how a magnet works? Well, without being too technical, a magnet is a piece of metal — usually iron, steel, cobalt or nickel — which has been charged with a magnetic field so that it attracts other particles of like metals. I have with me a magnet. Now, if I pass this over the spot where other bits of metal are, what do you think will happen? Let's try it! See, the smaller bits just jump onto the magnet and even larger pieces hold on tight. It is even possible for a magnet to be so strong that it is hard for a bit of metal to escape from its grasp. There are lots of ways in which magnets are used in our everyday world, such as electric motors, but we're not here to talk about that today. What I wanted you to see was the power of attraction, or the ability of the magnet to draw things to itself.

There is a passage in the Bible where Jesus speaks of his death on the cross in that way. He said that when He was lifted up off the earth, He would draw all men to himself. And over the centuries since He died on Calvary's cross, that is what has happened. Men and women, boys and girls, have been drawn to Jesus. We have learned of God's love for us and of the sacrifice that Jesus made to bring us back to God, and to be forgiven of sin. We have wanted to come to him. We are still drawn by Jesus to himself, and that is evident in the fact that we come here to this place to praise and worship him.

I hope our experiments with this toy magnet will serve to remind you of how God draws us to himself through the cross of Jesus. *(Prayer of thanksgiving for the work of Jesus on the cross.)*

40
Worldwide Christian Fellowship

Psalm 33:12: Blessed is the nation whose God is the Lord.
Proverbs 14:34: Righteousness exalts a nation.
Matthew 28:19: Go and make disciples of all nations.
Galatians 3:8: All nations shall be blessed in you.

Object: Tiny national flags (available on toothpicks in party shops). This may be used for the celebration of World Communion, Universal Day of Prayer, or World Peace Sunday, or as a story about Christian worship all around the world.

Good morning, boys and girls. Today in churches all around the world, people are doing something in common, regardless of nationality or different denominational creeds. Can anyone tell me what it is that millions of Christian people are doing together? *(Response.)*

That means that all around the globe, at different hours in the different time zones, Christian people are expressing the fact that they are all one in response to God and in remembering his son, Jesus.

Do you know someone who lives in a different part of the world who is a Christian? *(Responses — Allow several to tell of their overseas friends or of a relative who lives in a different time zone.)*

Would you like to be a part of a celebration today that will remind us of how we are connected to other people in the world today who are also Christians and are celebrating the same thing in their churches as we are here?

Okay, I'm going to give each of you a little flag to represent different nations of the world. *(Pass out flags.)* Now I want you to stand in a big circle with your flags in your right hands. *(If group is too big to make one circle, divide group into units of 6 or 8.)* Now let's sing "Jesus Loves The Little Children," and when we get to

73

the part where we say, "... red or yellow, black or white ..." let's raise our arms and hold our flags up high over our heads. *(Sing song together through twice.)* Now, children, let's pray and remember all the children of the world, many who have very special needs today.

41
Sacrificial Giving

Mark 12:43: The poor widow put in more than all the rest.

Object: A small coin (farthing, denari, halfpenny, smallest you can find)

Good morning, boys and girls. What does it mean to be poor? *(Responses — Hungry, poor clothing, homeless, no toys, no money.)* Do you know any poor people? *(Response.)* Do you think God loves poor people? *(Response.)* How does He help them? *(Response.)* Do you think that poor people love God? *(Response.)*

Sometimes people think that if they are very rich and buy things for the church or give a lot of their money to help other people, it shows how much they love God. The amount of money that we have to give is not always the best measure of our love for God.

Jesus was sitting outside the treasury building watching people as they gave money for the work of the temple. Lots of rich people put in large sums of money. Then a widow came along and put in two small copper coins. That doesn't sound like much, does it? Look at the little coin I have in my hand. You couldn't buy anything with it.

But Jesus said, "This woman has put in more then anyone because while they gave of their extra money, she, in her poverty, gave all she had to live on."

The lesson that we can learn from this story is that it isn't necessarily how much you give, but what it costs you to give it. A small gift given through sacrifice is of more value than a large gift which really doesn't cost much to the giver.

When you see a little coin, remember the widow's mite.

(Prayer to help us learn how to love God and help the poor.)

42
Giving Thanks

Genesis 8:22: While the earth remains, seed time and harvest ... shall not cease.
Matthew 9:37: The harvest is plentiful, the workers few.

Object: Candy corn or pumpkins

Good morning, boys and girls. How many of you have ever been to a county fair, or a carnival, or a festival? *(Responses — Some experience will be expressed.)* Isn't it fun? I love fairs and festivals. There is always so much to do and to see.

From the earliest records of history, we learn that people got together to celebrate special events in their lives. Do you know what one of the earliest celebrations was? *(Responses — Many good ideas may come. Acknowledge them.)* Men and women and boys and girls came together to celebrate the harvest!

The harvest was very important to primitive people who lived off the land because, if their crops failed, they would not be able to survive. Harvest is still important for those reasons today throughout the world, although we might not be aware of it since we are used to eating preserved or processed food. Still, if the harvest isn't made each year, the world and its people would soon starve. There are some places even today where a little crop failure means starvation for many people, even many little children.

As the grain harvests usually come in the autumn of the year, this is the season that we celebrate our (Harvest Festival, or Thanksgiving Service.) Corn and pumpkins are good symbols of the harvest season and also remind us that Halloween comes in the midst of our harvest time.

Let's pray a prayer of thanks to God for the rich harvest that He supplies us. *(Pray.)*
(Give out candy corn or pumpkins.)

43

Opening Your Heart To Jesus

Revelation 3:20: Behold, I stand at the door and knock.

Object: Picture cards — Sallman's *Christ at the Door* (It would be a helpful visual aid if you have available a door knocker to show to the children. The older or more unique, the better.)

Good morning, boys and girls. Does anyone know what this object is? *(Response.)* It is a door knocker. How many of you have door knockers on your house? *(Response — Some may.)*

I suppose that most people have electric doorbells attached to their homes nowadays. But long before the electric doorbell was invented, it was very common for people to have big door knockers. Some were made of heavy iron and many were made of shiny brass. People were often very proud of this sentinel at their door, and they made or bought ones that said something about their trade or their names or something that they liked especially well — like a pet.

One of the most often printed pictures in Christian art is this picture of Jesus knocking on a door. *(A large size copy would be helpful here. Talk a little about the picture.)*

Why do you suppose Jesus is knocking on that door? *(Responses — He wants to find out if anyone is home, He wants in, and so forth.)* Those are probably all good reasons, but the man who painted the picture was trying to give us a visual image of a verse that is in the Bible. Let me read it to you. *(Read Revelation 3:20.)*

(Depending on your purpose or where and how this message is used, here you might make a personal appeal to children to open their hearts to receive Jesus as Lord and Savior. The application at this point is very personal and I leave it to you.)

(Prayer that we might be responsive to Jesus when He wants to come into our lives and be with us.)

(Give each child a wallet card of Sallman's Christ at the Door. *They come with various texts or calendars on the reverse side.)*

77

44

The Just Live By Faith

Romans 1:17: The just shall live by faith.

Object: Martin Luther stickers or monk stickers

Good morning, boys and girls. Do you have bulletin boards at your school? *(Response.)* What are they used for? *(Responses — To tell you what's going on, for putting up posters, for leaving lost and found notices, and so forth.)* Do you ever read them? What's the most interesting thing you've ever read on the school bulletin board? *(Responses — take two or three.)* We have bulletin boards at the church, too, where we put up lots of information that we think is helpful for people who are active in the life of our church.

Now I want to tell you about a rather unusual bulletin board that played a very important part in the history of the world.

Back in the 1500s, more than 450 years ago, when someone had an important statement to make or wanted to call the attention of the people to an event, the person would nail or tack the announcement to the door of the church. It was usually at the center of the town and was a sure place to get it noticed.

On October 31, 1517, a priest by the name of Martin Luther, who was a professor at the University at Wittenberg, Germany, nailed a thesis — that is, a list of questions that he wanted to debate with others — to the door of the church where he preached.

He had serious questions about what the church taught about faith in contradiction to the things that he was studying in the Bible.

That simple act of nailing a notice to the church door started a chain of events throughout the churches of Europe that caused many people to leave the Roman Catholic Church and start different churches based on their understanding of the Bible. We call this period "The Reformation."

Martin Luther taught his followers that mankind should live before God by faith and not on the basis of doing good works to earn their salvation.

Today when we celebrate Reformation Sunday, we are remembering Martin Luther and all those who have stressed the importance of the Bible as the basis for our religious beliefs.

(Prayer that we might be diligent to study our Bibles and to have the courage to stand up for what we believe.)

(Give each child a sticker.)

45

The Heavens Declare

Genesis 1:1: God created the heavens and the earth.
Psalm 19:1: The heavens declare the glory of God.

Object: Star and moon stickers

Good morning, boys and girls. Have you ever been out on a clear dark night and spent time looking up at the sky? Some people, whom we call astronomers, spend their lifetimes studying the skies. Have any of you ever looked through a telescope? It enables you to see many more stars and planets than you can see with your naked eye.

When I was young, I remember lying on the grass and looking up into the dark sky. I saw thousands of little sparkles in the sky. It made me feel very little indeed. I began to wonder about the stars. They are so far away. I wondered why there are so many of them and how far away they are and how big they are. And the more I wondered about those twinkling stars, the more I began to marvel at God's creation. I remembered that it was his hand that created them all, even the ones I could not see or that have not even been discovered by mankind.

I believe it must have been an experience very much like that which caused the psalmist, David, to write a song about the stars in the heavens. Maybe as a little boy on the hillsides outside Bethlehem he looked up and wondered.

Isn't it fun to think that the same kind of experience he had so long ago is still available to us! God reveals himself to us in his creations today.

The most exciting thing about seeing all of those stars is that the Bible tells me that the God who created them loves us even more than He does them. When I think about that, I don't feel so small anymore, but I feel very special.

The sticker may remind you to have a look at the heavens and see the glory of God's creation. *(Pass out stickers.)*

(Prayer of thanks to God for all the ways He reveals himself to us in his creation.)

46

Don't Blow Your Own Horn

Matthew 6:2-3: When you give, do not announce it with trumpets.

Object: Toy trumpets or trumpet stickers

Good morning, boys and girls. Do you know what a braggart is? *(Response — Allow some free expression here.)* I suppose we have all known someone at some time who spent too much time telling us all about his or her accomplishments, haven't we? Maybe we can even remember a time or two when we bragged a little too much ourselves. We often do that because we want to feel important or because we want to impress someone. Often it works just the other way around and it makes people think we are trying to make ourselves better than others.

You know what really makes people feel good about you and respect you? It is when they find out something nice about you without your telling them.

Sometimes people do good deeds because they want to have others applaud them. Jesus taught people that when good deeds are done for that purpose, then that is the reward. But when good deeds are done to glorify God, He will reward the doer in heaven. He said, "When you do good or give gifts, don't announce it with trumpets." I suppose we translate that into the simple phrase, "Don't blow your own horn!"

God gives us all abilities to serve others and do good and kind acts for other. He knows when we are being faithful servants of his and doing our good deeds. We don't have to brag about how good we are or blow trumpets to announce our deeds — just do them!

(Give the object.)

(Prayer that we might be about our Father's business without fanfare.)

47
Faith Of Our Fathers

Psalm 33:12: Blessed is the nation whose God is the Lord.

Object: Pilgrim's hat (can easily be cut out from black paper)

Good morning, boys and girls. Have you ever sung the hymn "Faith of our Fathers"? *(Or, This morning we sang together the hymn "Faith of our Fathers.")*

Do you know who our fathers are? *(Responses — prior generations, grandparents, apostles, disciples, people who have lived before us, founders of our nation, and so forth.)* Well, I'm thinking this morning of a particular group of people who came to America in a little ship.

Anybody want to have a guess? Yes, they were the Pilgrims! And who can tell me the name of their ship and where they landed? *(Mayflower — Plymouth.)* Have any of you ever been to Plymouth and gone aboard the Mayflower II which sailed here from England in 1970 to mark the 350th anniversary of the first landing?

One of the interesting things that the Pilgrims did before they left their ship was to draw up a paper that stated what the government of their new land would be. That document, known as the Mayflower Compact, is one of the foundational papers of our national constitution.

Do you know why the Pilgrims came to the American shores? *(Response — The primary cause was to obtain freedom of worship though other answers may be a credible part of their history.)* The Pilgrims, or Puritans as they were known in England, had suffered religious persecution at home and they sought freedom in a new land. They wrote a principle of freedom of religion and conscience into their charter as they established their new colony. That principle of religious freedom is still very much alive in our country, and it is one of the things that we give thanks to God for in our annual Thanksgiving Day services.

This little hat will remind you of the Pilgrims and, I hope even more that, it will remind you of the precious religious freedoms that we enjoy in our nation.

(Prayer of Thanksgiving for the faith of our fathers and mothers.)

48
The Word Of God

Psalm 119:105: Thy word is a lamp to my feet.
John 8:51: If anyone keeps my word.
Colossians 3:16: Let the word of Christ dwell within you.
1 John 1:1: The Word of life.

Object: Tiny Bibles or Bible stickers

Good morning, boys and girls. Have you ever been in a really dark place? Did you think it was scary? What do you like to have with you when you know you are going into dark places? *(Responses — light, flashlight, candle, and so forth.)*

We have it very easy now, don't we? We have lights most places so that we don't have to live in the dark. Even when we go camping or into strange places, we have lights we can carry in our hands like this one *(produce flashlight)* that we can use to light our way.

It wasn't always like that. Many years ago, people had to rely on oil lamps or candles to find their way in the dark.

In a museum in St. Augustine, Florida, there is a display which shows a Chinese man who had a hole drilled in his head so that he could place a candle there to light his way. Isn't that strange? In ancient days, people had another way of carrying light with them to light their paths. They made little candle holders that fit onto their toes. When they walked, the light from the candle shone on their path. Wasn't that a clever idea?

The psalmist, David, must have had that in mind when he wrote Psalm 119 and spoke about the Word being a lamp to light his path.

What is the Word that David referred to in that Psalm? Does anyone know? *(Response — the Bible.)*

Yes, and how does the Bible become a lamp to help light the path for us? *(Responses — teaches us how to act, what to do, where to go in life, and so forth. Use these remarks to tie the principle of Bible guidance together.)*

(Prayer for illumination from the Word of God.)
(Give out the tiny Bibles or Bible stickers.)

49

The Bethlehem Star

Matthew 2:1-2, 9-10: The Wise Men followed the star.

Object: Large silver star stickers

Good morning, boys and girls. *(It may be appropriate to say a few words about the meaning of Advent or Epiphany.)*

One of the most interesting and familiar stories about what happened at the birth of the baby Jesus is told to us by Matthew. It is the story about a special star and of a group of men who were led by it to where the young child was. We even sing a song about these men. Who knows the name of the song? *(Response — "We Three Kings.")*

The three men were known as Magi. They were followers of a man named Zoroaster, and they were astronomers. Can you tell me what an astronomer is? *(Response — You may get some guesses but someone will say it's someone who studies the stars.)*

These men were wise. They not only studied the stars, they also studied the writings of the prophets. They knew that a new leader was to be born to Israel, and they wanted to come and worship him.

When they followed their special star, do you know what happened? *(Response.)* Yes, it led them right to the place where Jesus was, and they presented very precious gifts to him out of their joy and respect.

We may not have special stars in the sky to lead us to Jesus today, but we can find our way to him, too. The Bible tells us all about who Jesus was and is, and what He did when He came into the world. We can come to him in faith and receive him as the King of our lives today, even as wise men did so many centuries ago.

(Prayer to encourage us to seek Jesus in our lives today.)

(Give them a star to remind them of the Wise Men and the star of Bethlehem.)

50

Obedience And Grace

2 Corinthians 2:9: Obedient in all things.

1 Peter 1:14: As obedient children, do not be conformed to former things.

Object: Lumps of coal

Good morning, boys and girls. There is a very old custom which is associated with Christmas Eve. We always did it in our family even when we didn't have a proper fireplace. Can you think of what custom this is? *(Response — hanging stockings.)* Do you do that in your home? And what sort of things do you find in your stocking on Christmas morning? *(Response — Allow some freedom of expression.)* I always had trouble getting to sleep on Christmas Eve because I was so excited about the little treasures that I would find in my stocking in the morning.

Well, what would you say if you awoke on Christmas morning, full of excitement and anticipation, to find that the only thing in your stocking was a black lump of coal?

I remember hearing stories as a child about how disobedient or naughty children only received a lump of coal in their stockings on Christmas morning. I always half expected that to be my fate.

Aren't you glad that what you receive on Christmas Day has very little to do with whether you deserve it or not? Some of us would be in real trouble if we only got what we deserved, wouldn't we?

Do you know that the greatest gift that all the people of the world received was something that we didn't deserve? Who can tell me what that greatest gift was? *(Response — Jesus.)*

Yes, the Bible tells us that God sent his Son into the world to bring us salvation. That is, to save us from our sins, our disobedience, and our rebellion. It was not because we deserve it, but because He loved us. The great gift of Christmas is grace — God giving us his wonderful gift of love.

Let's remember, as we approach this Christmas, that it is important that we be obedient and well behaved, not so that we can avoid the lumps of coal in our stockings, but because that is how we respond to God's great act of love, and to the love that our parents give us so freely.

(Prayer of thanks for God's gift of grace.)

This lump of coal I have for you today is not because you have been naughty, but just as a reminder that God always gives us good gifts.

(Pass out coal.)

51

Angels Announce A Birth

Matthew 4:6: Give his angels charge over you.
Hebrews 13:2: Some have entertained angels unawares.

Object: Angel stickers or tree ornaments

Good morning, boys and girls. Has anyone here ever seen an angel? *(Responses — Some may relate to pictures or statues of angels.)* Well, does anyone know what an angel looks like? *(Responses — Wings, long hair, and so forth.)*

It is interesting that we know so little about angels when there are so many stories about them in the Bible. Let me share with you some of the things that we do know about them.

There are multitudes of angels — without number. It appears that God may have assigned one of them to watch over each one of us. That means that some of them must have to work awfully hard, doesn't it? Sometimes they have appeared like people and there may even be times when we have entertained them and not known they were with us. Angels are spiritual beings, a creation of God, and therefore may not be seen at times by the natural eye. There have been good and bad angels as well.

Yes, we know a lot about angels even though for most of us they are mysterious beings confined mostly to our reading about them in scripture.

Well, what do angels do? *(Responses — Take care of us, rejoice in heaven, make announcements for God.)*

The word "angelos" means messenger. And especially at this time of year, that is how we think of them. Angels came to Mary and Joseph, to Zechariah (the father of John the Baptist), and to shepherds on the hills outside Bethlehem. They came to announce the coming of the Son of God to the world, and their message brought great tidings of joy to the world.

So it is that the message of the angels still comes to us in our Nativity celebration to tell us that a Savior has been born who is Christ Jesus the Lord. We are thankful for the message of the angels. *(Give out angels.)*

(Prayer: We welcome the good news of our Savior's birth and join with the angels in praising God and saying, "Glory to God in highest.")

52

Away In A Manger

Luke 2:1-7: The birth of Jesus.

Object: Manger scene or baby in a manger

Good morning, boys and girls. These are very happy days, aren't they, filled with excitement and expectation? There are festive decorations everywhere — in the shops, along the streets of towns and cities, and in our homes. Many of the decorations are symbols that remind us of the Christmas stories in the Bible. What are some of the stories in the Bible about Jesus' birth? *(Responses — Allow time for many stars, angels, wise men, manger scenes, and so forth.)*

One symbol that I always like to see is the manger scene with the little baby Jesus in a little feed box. What we really are celebrating at Christmas is his birthday, isn't it?

Have you ever had a little brother or sister born into your family? Do you remember how excited you were when you first saw the baby, and how happy you felt to touch it and hold it in your arms? Didn't it make you want to celebrate? Well, that's the way it was in Bethlehem. Jesus' parents were so happy with the baby that God had given them that they were able to praise God, even though they were only in a stable.

But there was even more celebration at that stable where Jesus lay, because God sent an angel to tell others. Shepherds in the fields were told that a Savior had been born to them and they came to see and rejoice. Later a group of kings came from the East with birthday presents, and they also rejoiced because they had been told that a new king had been born.

All of this joyful celebration comes down to us today, doesn't it? The trouble is that many people who celebrate at the holiday season have forgotten what they celebrate. They leave Jesus out of the birthday party. Would you like to be left out of your own birthday party?

Let's make sure that we keep Jesus, the Christ, in our Christmas this year and every year. The little baby was born to bring joy and peace to our hearts as we honor him as our Lord.

(Prayer of praise to God for giving us a Savior.)

Scripture Index

5:1	26	**Hebrews**	
5:22, 23	22, 31	13:2	51
6:7	20	13:5	32
6:14	12	13:20	7
Ephesians		**1 Peter**	
3:17	8	1:14	50
5:2	24	3:10	16
5:19	28		
		1 John	
Philippians		1:1	48
2:9	38	1:7	15
Colossians		**Revelation**	
3:16	28, 48	3:20	43

Special Days Index

Object Index

A helpful list of objects to be used with the 52 children's message in this book. They are listed by lesson number.

1. Calendar
2. Calendar
3. Peanut in the shell
4. Whale sticker
5. Plain white paper
6. Fish sticker or toy
7. Lamb sticker
8. Heart sticker
9. Baby pin
10. Candy hearts
11. Shamrock sticker
12. Pocket cross
13. Palm leaf
14. Angel, open tomb, or lily card
15. Eraser
16. Lips sticker
17. Bookmark, Psalm 23
18. Bookmark, Ten Commandments
19. Carnation
20. Ruler, Golden Rule imprint
21. Balloon or birthday candle
22. Smiley face sticker
23. Apostles' bookmark
24. "Jesus Loves Me" item
25. Magnetic compass
26. Key
27. Matchstick flag or flag sticker
28. Notes
29. U.S. pennies
30. Toy watch
31. Red or purple grapes or sticker
32. "Footprints" poem

33. Map of world or globe sticker
34. Shepherd's crook or picture
35. Imitation pearl
36. Toy tool
37. Blackboard toy
38. Sallman's *Head of Christ* card
39. Toy magnet
40. National flags
41. Small coin
42. Candy corn or pumpkins
43. Sallman's *Christ at the Door* picture
44. Martin Luther or monk sticker
45. Star and moon stickers
46. Toy trumpet or trumpet sticker
47. Pilgrim hat
48. Tiny Bible or Bible sticker
49. Large silver star
50. Lump of coal
51. Angel sticker or tree ornament
52. Manger scene or baby in a manger